IT'S A BUG'S LIFE

By Brian Johnson

BRIGHT
connections media

A World Book Encyclopedia Company

Bright Connections Media
A World Book Encyclopedia Company
233 North Michigan Avenue
Chicago, Illinois 60601
U.S.A.

For information about other BCM publications,
visit our website at
http://www.brightconnectionsmedia.com
or call 1-800-967-5325.

It's a Bug's Life
ISBN: 978-1-62267-003-1

Printed in China by Toppan Leefung Printing Ltd.,
Guangdong Province
1st printing July 2012

Acknowledgments
Front and back cover: © Lorelyn Medina, Shutterstock; © Shutterstock;
© Thinkstock; © Science Faction/SuperStock

Interior: © Shutterstock; © Thinkstock; © Science Faction/SuperStock;
© imagebroker/SuperStock; © Minden Pictures/SuperStock; WORLD
BOOK illustration; © David Cappaert, Michigan State University/Bug-
wood; CFIA

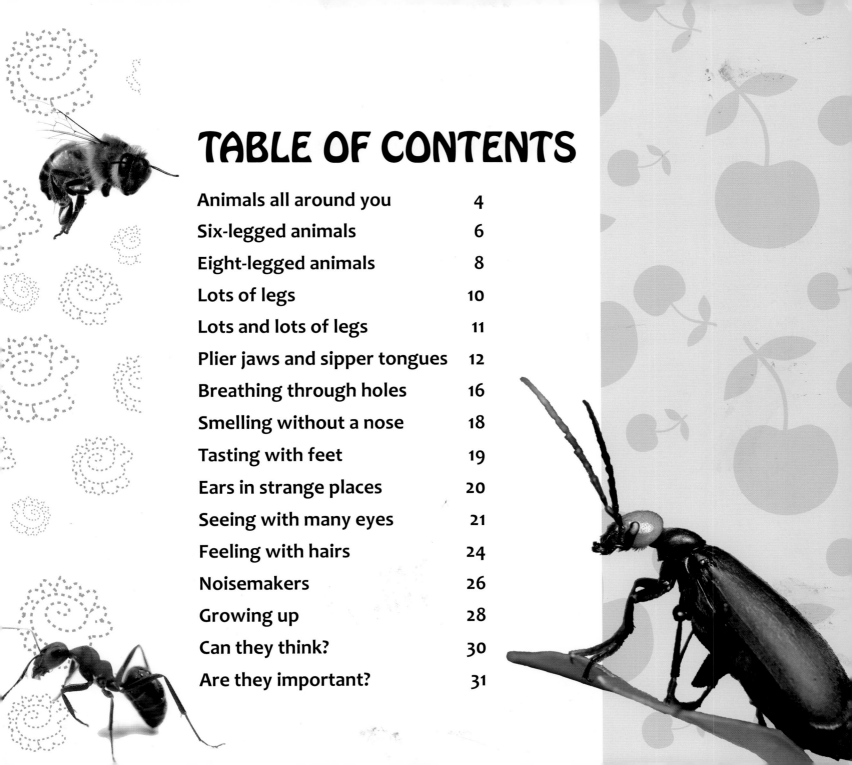

TABLE OF CONTENTS

Animals all around you 4

Six-legged animals 6

Eight-legged animals 8

Lots of legs 10

Lots and lots of legs 11

Plier jaws and sipper tongues 12

Breathing through holes 16

Smelling without a nose 18

Tasting with feet 19

Ears in strange places 20

Seeing with many eyes 21

Feeling with hairs 24

Noisemakers 26

Growing up 28

Can they think? 30

Are they important? 31

ANIMALS all around you

Have you ever wanted to watch wild animals up close? Well, you can! And you don't have to go to a zoo, or to Africa, or to the rain forests of South America. Just go to your own backyard or to a place with grass, bushes, trees, and water. Believe it or not, many wild animals live very close to you.

butterfly

caterpillar

Keep your eyes open. You will find animals that crawl like snakes when they are babies but have wings and fly when they grow up. You'll find fierce hunters that chase their prey. You'll see other hunters that lie in wait, make clever traps, or use disguises to get their meals. You'll even find animals that build "cities," have "farms," and keep herds of other animals!

4

All these creatures are the tiny animals we often call **"bugs."** But it's a mistake to call them all by this name. They are really different kinds of animals—each kind with its own name.

You may not have paid much attention to these tiny animals before. If not, you will be amazed to discover how strange and marvelous they truly are. They are also important. Many of these tiny creatures play a big part in our lives—even though we may not know it.

So turn the page and start to find out about the many kinds of tiny wild animals that are all around you. Learn about their ways of life and the amazing things they do. Then, go out and see them do the things you've read about.

ants

dragonfly

house fly

beetle

grasshopper

SIX-LEGGED animals

When the weather is warm, you see many tiny creatures buzzing about in the air, scurrying along the sidewalk, prowling through grass, and creeping over leaves. Most of these little creatures are the animals we call insects.

green swallowtail butterfly

ant

The rhinoceros beetle gets its name from its rhinoceros-like horn.

All insects have six legs. And every insect has a body with three parts—a head, a middle part, and a back part. If you touch an insect, it feels stiff and hard. This is because its body and legs are covered with hard skin. Most insects have feelers on their head. Most insects have wings, but some do not.

feeler

head

middle

body

honey bee

ladybug

There are more than a million kinds of insects, and scientists discover thousands of new insects each year. Ants, beetles, bees, butterflies, and grasshoppers are some of the insects you see most often.

EIGHT-LEGGED animals

The name of the exotic banana spider comes from the fact that they are sometimes found in bunches of bananas imported from such warm places as Central America.

Do you think a spider is an insect? It's not! A spider is a very different kind of animal than an insect.

Spiders belong to the group of animals called arachnids (uh RAK nihdz). Arachnids have eight legs. True insects have only six. The body of an arachnid is divided into two parts rather than three like an insect. No arachnid has wings or feelers.

daddy longlegs

scorpion

Like insects, arachnids have a hard skin. This hard skin may cover the whole body or only a part of it. For example, a spider's legs and front part are covered with an armorlike skin. But its back part is usually rather soft.

There are more than 50,000 kinds of spiders. And there are more than 30,000 other kinds of arachnids. Among the best known of the other arachnids are scorpions and daddy longlegs.

Lots of LEGS

wood louse

Wood lice, also called sow bugs or pill bugs, are not at all like insects or arachnids. These little creatures may have as many as 14 or 16 legs. Like many insects, they have feelers. But they do not have wings.

Although they are called bugs, these tiny animals are actually crustaceans (kruhs TAY shuhnz). They belong to the same class as shrimps, lobsters, and crabs.

Most crustaceans live in salt water. Like you, they need oxygen to live. You get oxygen out of the air when you breathe. Your lungs take oxygen from the air and pass it into your blood. In this way, the oxygen gets to all parts of your body.

But crustaceans don't have lungs. Instead, they breathe either through their skin or through organs called *gills*. Gills take oxygen from water and pass it into the animal's bloodstream. Wood lice, like most crustaceans, breathe through gills. So, even though they live on land, they have to keep wet to breathe.

Wood lice are small, flat, oval-shaped creatures. They look a bit like tiny armadillos. And, like the armadillo, some of them curl themselves into a ball when they are disturbed. A wood louse that does this looks like a small, gray pill. For this reason, it is often called a *pill bug*.

LOTS
and lots of legs

millipede

Have you ever seen animals that look like worms with legs—lots and lots of legs? They may look like worms, but they're not worms. They are animals called centipedes *(SEHN tuh peedz)* and millipedes *(MIHL uh peedz)*.

centipede

Centipede means "hundred feet." But some centipedes have only 30 legs. Others have nearly 400. *Millipede* means "thousand feet." But no millipede has that many legs. Some have as few as 24. Others have more than 300 legs. One species has more than twice that many!

Centipedes and millipedes look alike, but they are really very different. Both have feelers on their head and both have a body that is divided into many sections. But a centipede has two legs—a pair—on each section of its body. A millipede has four legs—two pairs—on each section. The total number of legs each animal has depends on the number of body sections.

PLIER JAWS
and sipper tongues

Insects, arachnids, and other many-legged animals don't have the kind of mouth we do. Their mouth is just an open hole.

The locust (left) is a short-horned grasshopper—that is, a grasshopper that has short feelers. The long-horned grasshopper (above) has threadlike feelers that may grow longer than its body. Many kinds of long-horned grasshoppers are green, but some are black, brown, or gray.

12

Insects have special parts around their mouth to help them eat. The kind of mouthparts an insect has depends on the way the insect eats. Some insects, such as ants and dragonflies, chew their food. These insects have two strong jaws that stick out on each side of the mouth. These jaws work like a pair of pliers. With them, the insect tears off pieces of food, such as bits of a leaf.

The inner edges of the jaws are usually lined with little teeth that can grind and cut. The jaws work sideways, not up and down as yours do. If you could hear an insect chewing a bit of leaf, it would sound much like a person chewing celery!

Actually, chewing insects have two sets of jaws. Behind the chewing jaws there is another set of jaws. These jaws are somewhat like fingers. They reach out and take the chewed-up food from the front jaws. Then, the jaws move back and push the food into the animal's mouth.

The dragonfly grabs hold of its prey with its legs or jaws. It may eat the prey while flying. Its large compound eyes, which cover most of its head, enable it to see in different directions.

13

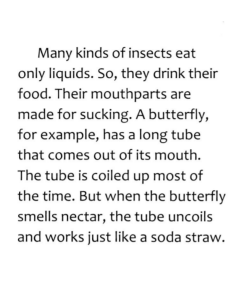

Many kinds of insects eat only liquids. So, they drink their food. Their mouthparts are made for sucking. A butterfly, for example, has a long tube that comes out of its mouth. The tube is coiled up most of the time. But when the butterfly smells nectar, the tube uncoils and works just like a soda straw.

This prepona butterfly sips food through a long tube that comes from its mouth. Many insects have such sipping tubes.

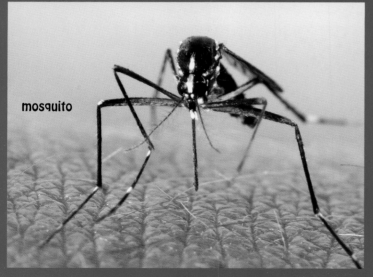

mosquito

A mosquito's lower lip contains a long beak with a groove in it. Six sharp "needles" stick out from the end of the beak. The mosquito jabs the needles into the skin of an animal or person, causing blood to flow. Then it sucks up the blood through the groove in its beak. Some kinds of insects suck juice from plants in the same way.

A house fly's lower lip forms a tube with a pair of thick pads on the end. The house fly sops up liquid with the pads and sucks the liquid up into its mouth. It can also turn some things, such as sugar, into liquid, so it can eat them. To do this, it lets "spit" ooze out of its mouth onto the food. This "spit" turns the solid food into a liquid.

house fly

All spiders have fangs on either side of their mouths. All except a few have poison glands. They use their fangs and poison glands to kill prey. A spider's bite can paralyze or kill insects and other small animals.

Spiders turn all of their food into liquid. They first kill their prey by crushing it or poisoning it. Then, as the spider sucks the food up through its mouth tube, a special liquid dissolves it.

BREATHING
through holes

Inside your chest is a pair of "bags" called lungs. They are much like balloons. When you breathe in, your lungs get larger. This causes them to pull in air. When you breathe out, your lungs get smaller. The air in your lungs is forced out.

An insect doesn't breathe this way. It has no lungs. An insect has a row of little holes on each side of its body. Fresh air seeps into the insect's body through the holes. The air moves about in the insect through a lot of little tubes. The "used-up" air goes back out through the holes in the insect's sides.

Caterpillars and other insects breathe through little holes in their sides.

Most kinds of spiders have one pair of lungs, but some have two pairs. A spider's lungs don't work the way your lungs do. Air gets into the lungs through one or two pairs of holes on the spider's underside.

Of course, insects, spiders, and all the other many-legged animals take in fresh air for the same reason you do. They need a gas, called oxygen, that's in air. The bodies of most living creatures use oxygen as a kind of fuel. Without it, they couldn't live.

17

SMELLING
without a nose

A luna moth skims lightly through the air on pale green wings. It is following a smell that may come from as far away as a mile.

The moth isn't sniffing the odor with its nose—it doesn't have a nose. It smells by means of many tiny, hairlike things on its two lacy, feathery feelers, or antennae.

Most of the many-legged animals that have feelers use them for smelling. Some kinds of insects also have "smellers" on their mouthparts. And some kinds of insects, as well as spiders, have smellers on their feet. A spider can follow a scent by walking on it!

TASTING with feet

You can't tell if something tastes good by putting your foot on it—but a fly can.

Flies, and several other kinds of insects, taste with their feet! When a fly lands on and walks across the potato salad, it's doing a taste test! When it steps on something that tastes good, it stops to eat.

Other insects, such as ants and bees, taste with their feelers. When you were on a picnic, did an ant ever touch your sandwich with its feelers? It was probably trying to find out if the sandwich was good to eat.

Insects that chew their food taste with their jaws. They taste their food best when they begin to chew it, just as we do. If something doesn't taste good, the insect stops chewing and gets rid of what it is eating.

EARS

in strange places

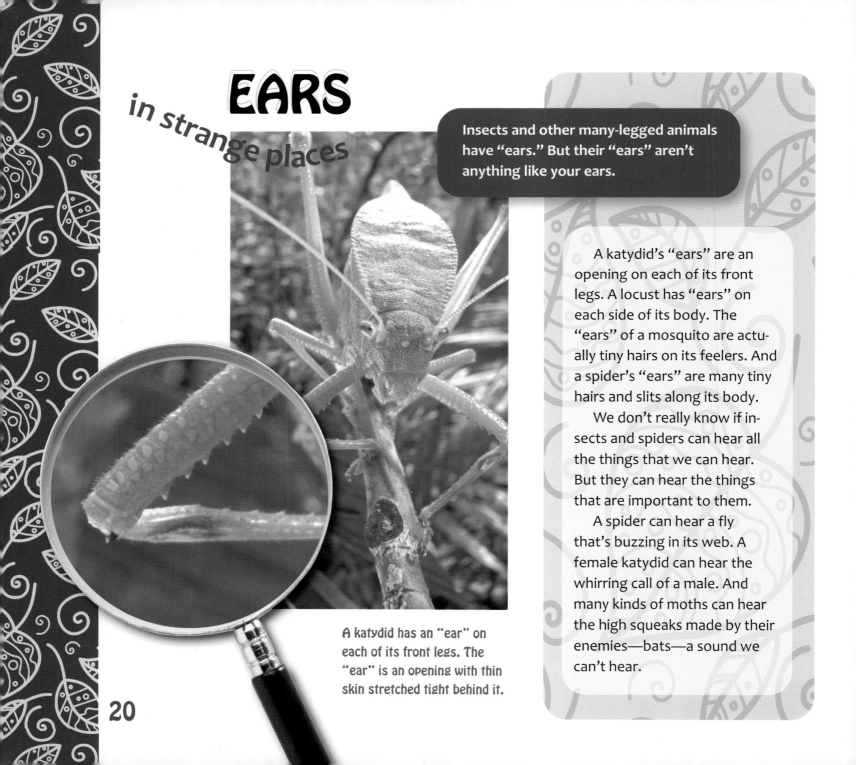

A katydid's "ears" are an opening on each of its front legs. A locust has "ears" on each side of its body. The "ears" of a mosquito are actually tiny hairs on its feelers. And a spider's "ears" are many tiny hairs and slits along its body.

We don't really know if insects and spiders can hear all the things that we can hear. But they can hear the things that are important to them.

A spider can hear a fly that's buzzing in its web. A female katydid can hear the whirring call of a male. And many kinds of moths can hear the high squeaks made by their enemies—bats—a sound we can't hear.

A katydid has an "ear" on each of its front legs. The "ear" is an opening with thin skin stretched tight behind it.

20

Seeing with many EYES

Suppose, for a moment, that you could see the world through the eyes of a many-legged animal. What do you think things would look like? Certainly, they would look very different. The eyes of an insect are not like our eyes. And most spiders see things through many eyes! What can that be like?

An insect's eyes are actually made up of many tiny eyes, as this close-up picture of a leaf bug shows.

Most insects have five eyes. Three of the eyes, which are on the insect's forehead, are very tiny and see only light. The other two eyes, which are on each side of the head, are enormous. These are the insect's main eyes.

Each main eye is made up of as few as 6 to as many as 30,000 tiny "eyes." So, instead of seeing one whole, clear "picture" as we do, an insect probably sees things as a great many pieces that fit together to form a single picture. Thus, things probably look rather blurry to an insect—like a newspaper picture when you look at it through a magnifying glass.

However, insects can probably see tiny movements better than we can. An insect's big eyes bulge out from its head. Because its eyes stick out, an insect can see ahead, on both sides, and even behind—all at the same time! It easily sees a movement anywhere around it. So it knows when something is trying to creep up on it. And hunting insects are able to find prey more easily.

Insects see some of the colors that we see, but other colors look different to them. A bee sees yellow, blue, violet, and bluish-green. But red looks green to a bee.

However, bees see some colors that we can't see. Scientists have found that some flowers have spots of color that are invisible to us. But bees and some other insects can see these colors.

Like many insects, the dragonfly has large, round eyes that let it see in all directions at once.

People see things "whole," like the flower shown at right. But insects probably see things in many little pieces, like the flower shown at far right.

A spider's eyes aren't like those of an insect. Most spiders have eight eyes. It is hard to imagine what things look like to a spider!

Some kinds of spiders have six eyes, like this wolf spider. Others have eight eyes.

Feeling with HAIRS

You feel with your skin. When you touch something, nerves in your skin tell you if the thing is hot, cold, wet, dry, smooth, rough, soft, hard, slick, or sticky.

An insect can't feel anything with its hard, armor-like skin. But insects have many tiny hairs growing out through their armor. They use these hairs to feel all the things we can feel.

Tarantulas, like other spiders, have hairs on their body that allow them to feel.

Insects have a great many of these "touch hairs" on their feelers. As an insect walks about, it "explores" everything with its feelers, touching them to everything it comes into contact with. With their feelers, many insects can tell how a thing feels, smells, and tastes—all at the same time!

So, an insect's feelers are very important. Often, you'll see an insect bend its head and rub its feelers with its front legs. It does this to clean its feelers. It cleans them by pulling them through a special sort of "comb" on its leg. This helps keep the feelers in good working order.

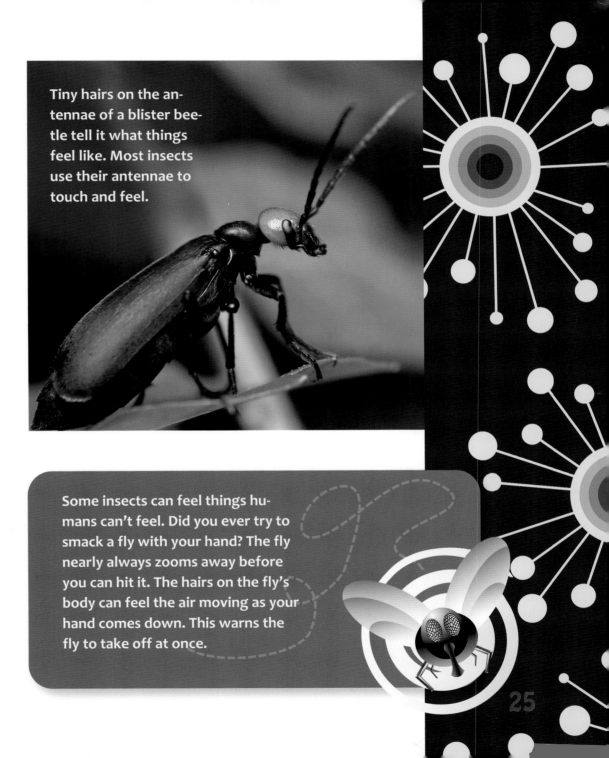

Tiny hairs on the antennae of a blister beetle tell it what things feel like. Most insects use their antennae to touch and feel.

Some insects can feel things humans can't feel. Did you ever try to smack a fly with your hand? The fly nearly always zooms away before you can hit it. The hairs on the fly's body can feel the air moving as your hand comes down. This warns the fly to take off at once.

NOISEMAKERS

Many insects are noisy! A fly can fill a whole room with a loud buzz as it soars and circles about. On a warm summer night, insects often keep up a steady chirp, creak, and whir. Do the noises *mean* anything? And how do the insects make these noises?

Some of the noises that insects make are not made on purpose. They just happen. The buzzing or humming sound that a flying insect makes is the sound of its wings moving very rapidly. For most insects, the sound doesn't mean anything. But for some insects, the sounds they make are important.

The sound made by a female mosquito's wings helps a male mosquito find her. A male can tell the sound of a female's wings even though there may be other noises around. By flying toward the sound, the male finds a mate.

Many of the chirps, creaks, and whirs of insects, however, are made on purpose. The insects make the noises by rubbing special parts of their bodies together, or by making a special part vibrate, or shake, rapidly.

Most of the sounds are made by male insects. They make use of some sounds to call females to them. A female goes toward the sound and finds the male. They mate, and in time she will lay eggs.

But some sounds mean other things. Some male crickets have special "territories" that they "own." If another male cricket comes into the territory, the "owner" makes a special noise that's a warning. It means, "Get out or I'll fight you!"

Often, a whole group of the same kind of insect will make the same kind of noise. This is a way of calling others of their kind, both males and females, to come to them. A grasshopper that's alone will head toward noise made by a group of others of its kind. This brings many grasshoppers together so they can find mates easily.

Insects aren't the only many-legged animals that make noise. Some kinds of male spiders also have special body parts they rub together to make noise.

Growing UP

Suppose you saw two flies standing close together. And suppose one fly was much smaller than the other. You would probably think the small one was a baby fly.

Actually, they would be two different kinds of flies. And both would be grown-ups. You can always tell a grown-up insect by its wings. Baby insects don't have wings. Baby insects aren't little creatures that look like their parents, as do many kinds of baby animals. Most baby insects don't look at all like their parents.

A fly begins life inside an egg that looks like a grain of rice. When the egg hatches, usually in a few hours, out comes the baby fly.

The baby fly doesn't look a bit like a grown-up fly. It has no wings, no feelers, and no legs. It looks like a tiny white worm. Many kinds of baby insects look like worms. Such wormlike babies are called **larvae** (*LAHR vee*).

Larvae don't do anything but eat and grow. But their skins don't grow, as ours do. A larva (*LAHR vuh*) grows *inside* its skin. When the skin becomes too tight, it splits open, usually down the back. Then the larva crawls out of the old skin! It may do this several times while it is "growing up."

A time comes when the larva has eaten enough and grown enough. Then it spins a silk covering, or forms a sort of shell around itself. Now it has become what is called a **pupa** (*PYOO puh*).

The young insect lies quietly inside its covering. Slowly, its body changes. It grows long legs and feelers. In most cases it grows wings—though some kinds of grown-up insects don't have wings. After some time it

The life cycle of a butterfly has many stages from caterpillar to adult.

breaks out of its covering. Now it has a body exactly like that of its parents. It has grown up. It will never grow any bigger.

Some kinds of insect babies, such as grasshoppers, are only a little different from their parents. They have legs and feelers. But they may have shorter, stubby bodies. And, at this age, they don't yet have wings. This kind of insect baby is called a **nymph** (*nihmf*).

A nymph is tiny when it comes out of its egg. It, too, grows by climbing out of its skin from time to time. Each time, its body gets a little bigger and its wings grow a bit. Finally, its wings swell up to full size. Now the insect is an adult. It will never grow any more.

Some kinds of wingless insects, as well as spiders, centipedes, and millipedes, have babies that look just like their parents. These babies, too, often **molt,** or shed their skin and grow a new one. Some kinds keep on growing all their lives. Even after they are adults, they shed their skin and get bigger from time to time.

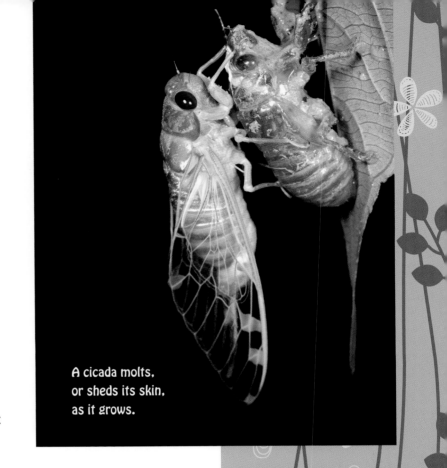

A cicada molts, or sheds its skin, as it grows.

Can they THINK?

When an insect comes out of its egg, it is ready for life. It knows what kind of food to eat and how to get it. It knows what certain sounds and smells mean. It doesn't have to learn any of these things. And it doesn't think about them. It is simply able to do them.

A honey bee can be taught to go to a color for food, such as this pink flower.

An insect's body contains many "messages." As the creature moves about, "messages" tell it what to do next. A certain smell may give it a message to taste. A certain taste will give it a message to eat. And so on. Most of the things an insect does are done because of these messages—not because the insect thought about doing them.

Some insects can learn things. A bee can be taught to go to a certain color for food. And some insects can remember things. A hunter wasp seems to find its way back to its nest by remembering landmarks. So insects have a kind of intelligence. But none of them can think as a human does—or even as well as a dog or cat does.

The hunter wasp finds its way back to its nest by remembering landmarks.

Are they IMPORTANT?

Insects are very important. They could get along without us—but we *couldn't* get along without them!

For one thing, insects and other many-legged creatures are important food for many fish, birds, and other animals.

Insects are just as important to many plants. Almost all fruits or vegetables begin as flowers. The flowers need pollen from another flower of its kind to develop. Insects, such as butterflies and bees, play a big role in carrying pollen from one flower to another.

Without insects, there wouldn't be many kinds of fruits and vegetables—such as apples, cherries, oranges, grapes, pears, carrots, cabbages, and onions! And, of course, all these kinds of plants would soon disappear, because there wouldn't be any seeds from which new plants could grow.

Many insects that live in the soil help keep the soil fertile so that plants can grow. Many kinds of insects and many-legged animals do important work as nature's garbage collectors. They feed on the remains of dead animals and plants.

Earthworms both fertilize and aerate (loosen) soil, making it suitable for plants to grow.

Several kinds of insects provide people with useful things. Honey, which is a very good food, is made by bees. Bees also make a wax that people use to make candles, shoe polish, furniture polish, and other things. Silk cloth is made from threads spun by certain kinds of caterpillars. Several kinds of medicine also come from parts of insects' bodies.

While some insects are helpful, we think of others as harmful. They damage plants and trees by eating parts of them or laying eggs in them. Many insects are a terrible problem for farmers. They destroy food. They also kill such useful plants as cotton. There are also insects that do great damage to wood, to cloth, and to such stored foods as flour, cheese, and meat.

Some insects carry germs that cause diseases. The disease called malaria (*muh LAIR ee uh*) kills at least a million people each year. Malaria is carried by a certain kind of mosquito. A certain kind of fly carries the disease called sleeping sickness. This disease is a serious problem in Africa. Even ordinary house flies can carry diseases, as can ticks, lice, and fleas.

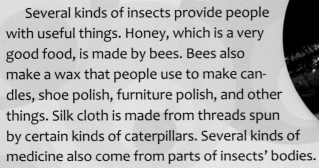

The emerald ash borer, a beetle accidentally imported from China, is killing millions of ash trees in North America. Its larvae bore into a tree, damaging the inner bark.

Insects are, indeed, important—some because they are useful to us; others because they cause serious trouble. But we shouldn't think of insects and other many-legged animals as "good" or "bad." Like all wild creatures, they are simply doing what they must to stay alive. They are part of the great web of life that includes every living plant and animal.